National curriculum

Level 3

activities based on:

'Clever cakes' & other texts

Kate Grant

Contents

	Page
Introduction	3
Week 1 Clever Cakes from *Clever Cakes and Other Stories* by Michael Rosen, illustrated by Caroline Holden	7
Week 2 Philibert the First from *Philibert the First and Other Stories* by Dick King-Smith, illustrated by Amanda Harvey	13
Week 3 The Hobyahs by Val Biro	19
Week 4 Instructions Party recipes	25
Week 5 Concrete poetry 'Orange' and 'Pineapple' by John Cotton, 'Earth-worm' by Leonard Clark; 'Inside the egg' by Noel Petty	31
Week 6 Explanation text Air pressure and windy weather (from *Weather and Climate* by Barbara Taylor)	37
Anthology	
Instructions for party recipes	43
Orange and Pineapple	44
Earth-worm	45
Inside the egg	46
Air pressure and windy weather	47

Author Kate Grant
Editor Alison Rosier
Assistant editor Roanne Davis
Series designer Paul Cheshire
Illustrations Chantal Kees

Designed using Adobe Pagemaker
Published by Scholastic Ltd, Villiers House, Clarendon Avenue, Leamington Spa, Warwickshire CV32 5PR
Text © Kate Grant
© 2000 Scholastic Ltd
1 2 3 4 5 6 7 8 9 0   0 1 2 3 4 5 6 7 8

British Library Cataloguing-in-Publication Data
A catalogue record for this book is available from the British Library.
ISBN 0-439-01829-3

The right of Kate Grant to be identified as the Author of this work has been asserted by her in accordance with the Copyright, Designs and Patents Act 1988.

All rights reserved. This book is sold subject to the condition that it shall not, by way of trade or otherwise, be lent, hired out or otherwise circulated without the publisher's prior consent in any form of binding or cover other than that in which it is published and without a similar condition, including this condition, being imposed upon the subsequent purchaser.

No part of this publication may be reproduced, stored in a retrieval system, or transmitted, in any form or by any means, electronic, mechanical, photocopying, recording or otherwise, without the prior permission of the publisher. This book remains copyright, although permission is granted to copy pages marked with the photocopiable icon for classroom distribution and use only in the school which has purchased the book or by the teacher who has purchased the book and in accordance with the CLA licensing agreement. Photocopying permission is given for purchasers only and not for borrowers of books from any lending service.

Acknowledgements

The publishers gratefully acknowledge permission to reproduce the following copyright material:

● **The Estate of Leonard Clark:** The Literary Executor of Leonard Clark for the use of 'Earth-Worm' by Leonard Clark from the anthology *Daybreak: A First Book of Poems* © 1963, The Estate of Leonard Clark (1963, Rupert Hart-Davis).

● **John Cotton** for the use of 'Orange' and 'Pineapple' by John Cotton from *Words, Whirls and other Shape Poems* edited by John Foster © 1998, John Cotton (1998, OUP).

● **Kingfisher Publications plc** for the use of the extract 'Air Pressure' from *Young Discoverers: Weather and Climate* © 1992, Grisewood and Dempsey (1992, Kingfisher Publications).

● **Jennifer Luithlen Agency**, agent for Val Biro, for permission to scan in illustrations from *The Hobyahs* by Val Biro © 1985, Val Biro (1985, OUP).

● **Oxford University Press** for the use of an extract from *The Hobyahs* by Val Biro © 1985, Val Biro (1985, OUP).

● **Peters Fraser and Dunlop** for use of illustrations by Amanda Harvey from *Philibert The First and Other Stories* by Dick King-Smith, Illustrations © 1994, Amanda Harvey (1994, Viking).

● **Noel Petty** for the use of 'Inside The Egg' by Noel Petty from *Madtail, Miniwhale and Other Shape Poems* edited by Wes Magee © 1989, Noel Petty (1989, Puffin).

● **Walker Books Ltd** for the use of text and scanned illustrations from *Clever Cakes* by Michael Rosen, Text © 1991, Michael Rosen, Illustrations © 1991, Caroline Holden (1991, Walker Books Ltd, London).

Every effort has been made to trace copyright holders for the works reproduced in this book, and the publishers apologize for any inadvertent omissions.

Introduction

Why do I need special needs resources for group time?
The National Literacy Strategy *Framework for Teaching* requires that all children's needs are catered for in the daily Literacy Hour. The class teacher can address individual needs through targeted questions and direct teaching in the first part of the hour when the whole class is taught. However, there is a real necessity for purposeful activities for children with special needs during the group/independent work section of the hour when the teacher is working elsewhere with guided reading/writing groups. This book is geared to allowing children with special needs to work at an appropriate level on relevant objectives under the guidance of a classroom assistant or other adult.

How does the book work?
Each of the chapters in this book contains five photocopiable lessons, designed to fit into the 20-minute group/independent work slot in the Literacy Hour and to be used by a classroom assistant or other additional adult. The lessons are based on particular texts, and children working on the activities will need access to them. The three story books are:
- *Clever Cakes and Other Stories* by Michael Rosen, illustrated by Caroline Holden (Walker Books)
- *Philbert the First and Other Stories* by Dick King-Smith, illustrated by Amanda Harvey (Viking)
- *The Hobyahs* by Val Biro (Oxford University Press)

The fiction texts should be familiar to the children, ideally from a guided reading lesson.
Non-fiction texts and poems are provided as photocopiable pages. One story or extract is the focus for each week's lessons; the activities are at text, sentence and word level and include writing frames and homework tasks.

How does it fit into the Literacy Hour planning?
The genre for the lessons is chosen from the range for Year 5 but the learning objectives are usually from previous years or terms, since children with special needs are still developing and practising skills from an earlier stage. In this way, if the class is studying novels by significant children's authors, for example, the chapter on *Philibert the First* could be selected for the group working with the classroom assistant.
The objectives are clearly indicated in the grid at the start of each chapter, allowing for simple group target-setting.

How flexible is it?
Each chapter in this book can be used independently – there is no need to follow any particular order. Although the texts have been selected to appeal to Year 5 children reading Level 3 texts, they may also be suitable for older children with learning difficulties who are working at this level. The materials can also be used outside the Literacy Hour for additional support if required.

Will classroom assistants need any training to use this book?
Everything that is needed to carry out the group-time lesson is explained in the straightforward notes for each day. There are also useful hints provided in the next few pages to help classroom assistants support children with reading, writing and spelling.

What is the range of the texts?
For Year 5/Level 3, the texts include:
- stories by significant children's authors (*Clever Cakes* by Michael Rosen and *Philbert the First* by Dick King-Smith)

- a traditional story (*The Hobyahs*)
- concrete poetry ('Orange', 'Pineapple', 'Earth-worm' and 'Inside the egg')
- an instruction text (Party recipes)
- an explanation text (Air pressure and windy weather)

What objectives are covered?
Learning objectives include:
- **Text level:** comprehension, characters, narrative sequence, story settings, preparation for factual research, writing a record of information, location of key words, identification of text features, writing instructions, reading and writing concrete poems
- **Sentence level:** verbs, adjectives, singular and plural, joining sentences, question marks
- **Word level:** alphabetical order, spelling by analogy, high-frequency words, new vocabulary, contracted words, synonyms, homonyms, silent *k*.

High-frequency words/spelling by analogy
The following lists show the high-frequency words and spelling patterns that can be focused on when you are using the texts in the activities. The high-frequency words are from the National Literacy Strategy List for Years 4 and 5.

	High-frequency words			Spelling patterns
Clever Cakes	outside	walk	inside	-eak
Philibert the First	other	morning	happy	-ead
The Hobyahs	great	never	can't	-le
Party recipes	until	leave	together	ge-
Concrete poems	half	suddenly	eyes	wor-
Air pressure and windy weather	earth	across	balloon	-eep

Reading
Before choosing a week's lessons, make sure that the text being used is at a suitable reading level (the children in the group should be able to read it with no more than one error in every ten words).

Fiction books: The lessons which use the story books as their basis assume that the story will already have been read by the children, either with the teacher in a previous guided reading lesson, or at some other time. If the children have not already read the book, introduce it in the following ways:
- Look at the cover and title – read the title, pointing to the words as you do so.
- Talk together about the author and illustrator, briefly.
- Look through the story together – look at the pictures, discuss what is happening but don't give away the ending at this stage.

   Ask the children to:
- find and read the characters' names
- tell you the story from the pictures
- find key words
- find difficult words and read them aloud together
- explain what some of the tricky words mean.

   When you read the story with the children, ask them sometimes to read a page as a group, sometimes in turn and sometimes silently. Ask a couple of questions to check

that they have understood the story on the pages they have read silently. Check that they are changing the expression in their voices and noticing speech marks and other punctuation.

Non-fiction/information texts: The lessons based on the non-fiction texts ('Party recipes' and 'Air pressure and windy weather') do not assume that the children will have read the text before. Although Day 1 explains how to introduce and read the text, it is helpful to bear in mind the following general points about introducing non-fiction texts:
- Ask the children to read some of the captions to the pictures and the headings for the different sections.
- Help the children to think of some things that the text might help them to learn about.

As with reading fiction, when the children read the text, ask them sometimes to read a section as a group, sometimes in turn and sometimes silently. Ask a couple of questions to check they have understood the parts they have read silently.

Poems: The children do not need to have seen the shape poems before you begin the lessons for Week 5. The notes for Day 1 explain how to introduce each poem but you could also help the children to consider how a poem looks different from a story or an information text, and make sure they know that there is a special term for the author of a poem (poet).

Helping children with reading

Ask the children to tell you how they can work out a word they are finding difficult to read. They could:
- go back to the beginning of the sentence
- say the first sound and think of a word that fits
- leave out the difficult word, read a few more words, then have another try
- look for a little word they know inside the difficult word, for example *l*and*ed*
- look for a pattern they know, for example *old* in sc*old*.

Remind the children of things they should ask themselves as they read:
- Does it make sense?
- Does it sound right?
- Does it look right?

Helping children with writing

The aim should be to enable the children to write as much as possible on their own, and your help will be geared to developing their skills. The writing frames provided in this book give the children a 'scaffold' so that they are not faced with a blank sheet of paper, but you will still need to discuss with them some ideas for what they might want to write. It is a good idea not to let them have pencils until you have finished a preliminary discussion. Have scrap paper or a dry-wipe board and pen available for trying out spellings.

If children ask you how to spell a common (or high-frequency) word that they will need to use fairly often, teach them to spell it by getting them to write it a few times using the Look–Say–Cover–Write–Check method (see page 6).

Another way to help is to draw boxes for the letters in the word (if it is one that can be 'sounded out' fairly easily.) Ask what they can hear at the beginning, middle and end of the word, then help them to put in the missing letters.

For example, if a child wants to write *rocket*, ask him or her to say the word. Once the child can hear the *r*, the *k* in the middle and the *t* at the end, you can help him or her to put the letters in the correct boxes.

| r | | k | | t |

Next, help the child to say the word again, emphasizing each sound so that he or she can hear more letters. You may need to explain that there is another letter that sounds the same as *k*. The *e* sounds like *i* so you may need to help with this letter, too. Eventually the whole word will appear in the boxes.

| r | o | c | k | e | t |

Encourage the children to keep on reading their sentences as they are writing them, so that they don't leave words out. Remind them to put in capital letters, full stops and so on, and make sure they read their writing through carefully when they have finished.

Supporting spelling (Look–Say–Cover–Write–Check)

If you train children to learn a new word by this method every time they want to remember a spelling, they will nearly always be successful.

> Have a good LOOK at the word.
> SAY the word and spell out the letters.
> COVER the word so that you can't see it.
> WRITE the word down.
> Uncover the word to CHECK if it's right.

The children should repeat the process as often as necessary until they get the word right three times running. Even if the spelling is forgotten later, they will probably have most of the letters right, and relearning will be much quicker the second time.

One reason this method works is because it uses three different ways to learn the same thing. You use your:
- **eyes** to look at the word
- **ears** to hear the letter names as you say them
- **hand** to write the word, and get the feel of its pattern and shape.

This gives the brain several chances to store the word in the memory.

It can help children's handwriting development as well as their spelling if they write the words in joined writing, so that they are learning the spelling patterns as a continuous movement.

Making spelling resources

Some of the activities in this book refer to the use of a word wheel and flick book. These can be made very easily and children really do enjoy using them.

Making a word wheel to learn spelling patterns

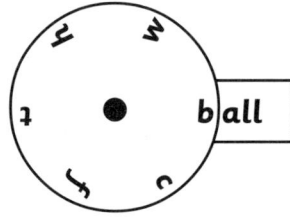 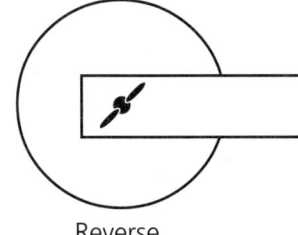

Reverse

Use a butterfly fastener in the centre of the card.

Making a flick book to learn spelling patterns

Staple here.

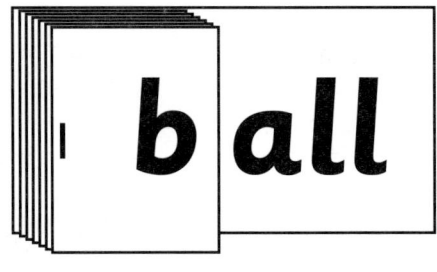

Write a different letter on each small piece of paper to make words, eg *wall*, *fall*, *tall* and so on.

Resources for Group Time
Support for Struggling Readers

Week 1 Clever Cakes

from *Clever Cakes and Other Stories* by Michael Rosen, illustrated by Caroline Holden

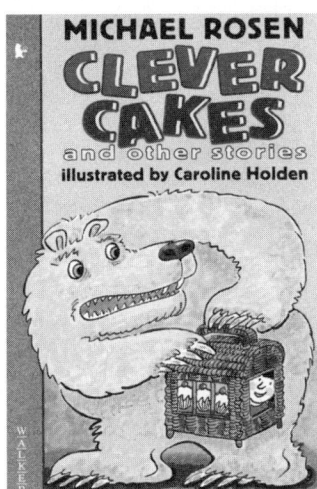

In *Clever Cakes and Other Stories,* Michael Rosen, the celebrated children's poet and author, has used the familiar theme of children cleverly outwitting dangerous or wicked characters. In the first story, Masha gets the better of a *massive muscly bear*, who is not terribly bright, by thinking on her feet. Children, as they read, enjoy being party to the trick Masha plays on the bear.

Reading such an accessible book of short stories can enable children to feel that they have entered the world of 'real chapter books'. If they enjoy reading this story with support in class, they can be encouraged to try reading other chapters for themselves.

Week 1 Objectives

	Word level	Sentence level	Text level
Day 1 Reading Chronology in narrative		To use awareness of grammar, phonic and graphic knowledge, word recognition and context when reading Y3 T2 (1)	To be aware of the different voices in stories Y3 T1 (3) To explore chronology in narrative Y4 T1 (3)
Day 2 Comprehension			To make sense of what they read Y2 T3 (2)
Day 3 Sight vocabulary Spelling by analogy	Spelling by analogy with other known words Y4 T1–3 (3)		
Day 4 Adjectives Silent *k*	To recall high-frequency words Y4 T1–3 (1)	To revise work on adjectives Y4 T2 (1)	
Day 5 Writing composition	To investigate, spell and read words with silent letters Y3 T2 (10)	How sentences can be joined Y3 T3 (5)	To begin to organise stories into paragraphs Y3 T1 (16)
Homework task 1 Questions and statements		To secure knowledge of question marks Y3 T1 (6)	
Homework task 2 True or false?		To use context when reading Y3 T3 (1)	

Day 1 — Week 1 Clever Cakes

Reading

The children should have already read this story with the teacher in guided reading. If they are not familiar with the book, follow the instructions for fiction books (see page 4) before beginning Day 1.

Ask the children to find a part of the story where either the bear or Masha was speaking. The children should practise reading their chosen dialogue, using the character's voice. Encourage them to put appropriate expression into their reading.

Chronology in narrative

Ask the children to read page 7 and find phrases that tell you when something happens in the story (*Once there was...* and *One day...*)

Explain that words and phrases like these in stories are often at the beginning of paragraphs. They help to link the parts of the story together. Help the children to find more examples of phrases that show how time is passing in the story.

page 8: *Then, very suddenly...; So now Masha had to...; all day long...*
page 10: *As soon as...;When he...*
page 11: *After a while...*
page 12: *But now...*
page 14: *When he got there...*
page 15: *As soon as...*

The children should choose one of these phrases to start a sentence and complete it in their own words.

Resources for Group Time

Day 2 — Week 1 Clever Cakes

Comprehension

Quiz (oral or written answers)
1. Who did Masha play with?
A. Her friends.
2. What game did Masha play with her friends?
A. Hide-and-seek.
3. Why did Masha shout *'Help!'*?
A. She was lost.
4. Where did Masha put the cakes?
A. In a basket.
5. When did Masha come out of the basket?
A. When the bear ran away.

Quiz (written answers)
1. Who did Masha live with?
A. Her granny.
2. Where did the bear think the voice was coming from?
A. The cakes.
3. Name one thing the bear wanted Masha to do.
A. Cook, clean, wash or scrub.
4. Was the bear enormous?
A. Yes.
5. How did Masha feel about keeping house for the bear?
A. She hated it.

Questions

Give each child a different question word, for example: *What, When, Where, Who, Why, How.*

The children think of a question about the story beginning with their word. Each child, in turn, asks the group to answer the question.

Resources for Group Time

Resources for Group Time
Support for Struggling Readers

Sight vocabulary

outside, walk, inside

Ask the children to find the word *outside* (on page 7) and to learn to spell the word using the Look–Say–Cover–Write–Check method (see page 6 of this book) until they can write it from memory. Do the same with *walk* (page 7) and *inside* (page 11). The children write the words in their spelling books to take home for further practice.

Help the children to think of a sentence with all three words in it, and to write it down, using a coloured pencil or felt-tipped pen to highlight *outside*, *walk* and *inside*.

Spelling by analogy

Spelling pattern: -*eak*

Ask the children to find *speak* on page 12 and to look carefully at the word. They should learn to spell the word using the Look–Say–Cover–Write–Check method (see page 6) until they can write it from memory.

Encourage them to think of other words that rhyme with *speak* (for example *leak, weak, beak, creak, peak*). Dictate the words for the children to write in their spelling books. Avoid words that rhyme but are spelled differently, for example, *week, seek, cheek*.

Dictate the following sentences for the children to write. (Decide whether or not you want them to have the word list for reference.) Remind them about capital letters, question marks and full stops, if necessary.

*Can a duck **speak** from its **beak**?*
*I am too **weak** to reach the **peak**.*

The children should underline all the *-eak* words in their completed sentences with a coloured pencil or felt-tipped pen. They could make word wheels or flick books with the spelling pattern to take home (see page 6).

Day 3 — Week 1 Clever Cakes

Resources for Group Time

Adjectives

Ask the children to find two words that describe the bear on page 8 (*massive, muscly*). Can they remember the name for words that describe things? (Adjectives.)

Help the children to find other adjectives that describe the bear on page 11 (*tired, hungry*) and page 14 (*horrible, great, greedy*).

Ask the children which of the adjectives describe how big the bear was. (*Great, massive.*) Help the children to list all the adjectives they can think of, that can be used instead of *big* (for example *huge, enormous, gigantic, large*).

Silent *k*

Ask the children to find *knew* on page 12. What sound can they hear at the start of *knew*? (*n*) Explain to the children that the letter *k* is silent, so that you can't hear it at the beginning of the word.

Encourage the children to think of other words that sound like *n* at the beginning but have a silent *k* (for example *know, knee, knock, knit, knobbly, knight*).

Make up a sentence together about a *knight* with *knobbly knees*. The children should write the sentence and highlight all the silent letters.

Day 4 — Week 1 Clever Cakes

Resources for Group Time
Support for Struggling Readers

Write a story

How does the story begin?

What happens first?

How does the problem arise?

What happens next?

How does the story continue?

How does the story end?

Writing composition:
Explain that the children are going to write a story where a child tricks an animal that wants to eat him or her. Each paragraph should start with a phrase linking it in time to the one before. (Remind the children of the activity on Day 1.)

Clever Cakes

Questions and statements

Can you change these statements into questions? The first one has been done for you.
Don't forget the question marks.

1 Masha played hide and seek with her friends.

   Why did Masha play hide and seek with her friends?

2 The bear was massive and muscly.

   _____

3 Masha came out of the basket.

   _____

4 Masha put the cakes in her basket.

   _____

5 Granny lived in a cottage in the woods.

   _____

6 Masha did not like looking after the bear.

   _____

7 The bear thought the cakes were talking.

   _____

   _____

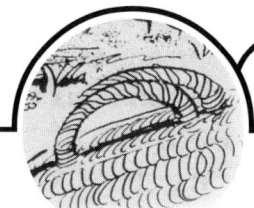

Clever Cakes

True or false?

Try to remember the story of 'Clever Cakes' and write down whether these sentences are true or false.

1 Masha lived with her mum and dad. _____

2 Masha and her friends played hide and seek. _____

3 The bear was very thin. _____

4 Masha had to do the bear's shopping. _____

5 The bear thought he was clever. _____

6 Grandma wasn't scared of the bear. _____

7 The cakes could talk. _____

8 Masha was less clever than the bear. _____

Week 2 Philibert the First

from *Philibert the First and Other Stories* by Dick King-Smith, illustrated by Amanda Harvey

Dick King-Smith is a very popular author of many books for children. 'Philibert the First', from his collection of short stories, is the story of King Philibert, who has not smiled or laughed for nearly a year despite living in the wonderful land of Felicia where everyone is happy. The Royal Vet finally solves the problem for both Philibert and his pet walrus, Norman.

Although the story is amusing and easy to follow, there are examples of descriptive passages, a wide use of vocabulary and sophisticated story-language which provide opportunities to develop the children's responses to narrative text.

Week 2 Objectives

	Word level	Sentence level	Text level
Day 1 Reading Setting Story language		To use awareness of grammar, phonic and graphic knowledge, word recognition and context when reading Y3 T2 (1)	To understand how writers create imaginary worlds through detail Y4 T2 (1) To investigate the styles and voices of traditional story language Y3 T2 (1)
Day 2 Comprehension Story themes			To make sense of what they read Y2 T3 (2) To identify typical story themes Y3 T2 (2)
Day 3 Sight vocabulary Spelling by analogy	Spelling by analogy with other known words Y4 T1–3 (3) To recall high-frequency words Y4 T1–3 (1)		
Day 4 Vocabulary extension Using a dictionary and thesaurus	To generate synonyms for high-frequency words Y3 T1 (17) To understand the purpose and organisation of the thesaurus Y3 T1 (16)		
Day 5 Writing composition			To develop the use of settings in own writing Y4 T2 (10)
Homework task 1 Vocabulary	To collect new words from reading Y3 T3 (12)		
Homework task 2 Wordsearch	To collect new words from reading Y3 T3 (12)		

Day 1 — Week 2 Philibert the First

Reading
The children should have already read this story with the teacher in guided reading. If they are not familiar with the book, follow the instructions for fiction books (see page 4) before beginning Day 1.

Setting
Tell the children they are going to 'make a picture in their heads' as you read the first two pages of the story together as a group.

Ask the children: *What is the setting?* or *Where does the story take place?* (The land of Felicia.)

Ask them to remember as much information as they can about the setting.

Encourage the children, in pairs, to write a list headed 'Life in Felicia'. These should be brief notes rather than sentences, for example, *No schools*.

Story language
Ask the children to:
- find these phrases in the text –

  Thus it was... (page 16)
  Now it so happened... (page 13)
  Oh what joy there was throughout the land... (page 19)

- think about what kind of text would have phrases like this (traditional stories, fairy tales and so on)
- find a phrase at the end of the story that is very common in traditional stories (*happily ever after*)
- suggest what traditional phrase could have been used at the beginning. (*Once upon a time...*)

Resources for Group Time

Day 2 — Week 2 Philibert the First

Comprehension

Quiz (oral or written answers)
1. Who was Norman?
A. The walrus.
2. What was Norman's favourite food?
A. Oysters.
3. What noise did Norman make when the new walrus arrived?
A. Vroom.
4. Think of a word starting with *g* that means the same as *unhappy*.
A. Gloomy.
5. Why should Norman not have eaten oysters in May?
A. No *R* in the month.

Quiz (written answers)
1. What day did everyone in Felicia have to work?
A. Friday.
2. When did it rain in Felicia?
A. At night.
3. What did Philibert say when he was asked why he was unhappy?
A. 'I don't know.'
4. How many daughters did Philibert have?
A. Three.
5. Who solved the King's problem?
A. The Royal Vet.

Traditional stories – problem and solution

Explain to the children that traditional stories often have a problem which someone has to solve. Ask them what the *problem* is in 'Philibert the First'. (The King is not happy.) What is the *solution* to the problem? (The Royal Vet finds a mate for the pet walrus.) Help the children to think of problems and solutions in other well-known stories. For example:
- 'Jack and the Beanstalk': problem – no money; solution – giant's bag of gold
- 'Cinderella': problem – can't go to the ball; solution – fairy godmother
- 'Sleeping Beauty': problem – asleep for 100 years; solution – prince's kiss wakes her.

Resources for Group Time

Sight vocabulary

other, morning, happy

Ask the children to find the word *other* (on page 9) and to learn to spell the word using the Look–Say–Cover–Write–Check method (see page 6 of this book) until they can write it from memory. Do the same with *morning* (page 10) and *happy* (page 8). The children should write the words in their spelling books to take home for further practice.

Help the children to think of a sentence with all three words in it, and to write it down, using a coloured pencil or felt-tipped pen to highlight *other, morning* and *happy*.

Spelling by analogy

Spelling pattern: -ead

Ask the children to find *head* on page 11 and to look carefully at the word. They should learn to spell the word using the Look–Say–Cover–Write–Check method (see page 6) until they can write it from memory. Encourage them to think of other words that rhyme with *head* (for example *bread, read, tread, spread, instead, thread*). If they suggest words such as *red, bed* or *said*, which rhyme but are spelled differently, explain that these words have a different spelling pattern so they do not fit in today's list. Dictate the *-ead* words for the children to write in their spelling books.

Dictate the following sentences for the children to write. (Decide whether or not you want them to have the word list for reference.) Remind them about capital letters, question marks and full stops, if necessary.

*The king **spread** jam on his **bread**.*
*I have **read** the story in my **head**.*

The children should underline all the *-ead* words in their completed sentences with a coloured pencil or felt-tipped pen. They could make word wheels or flick books with the spelling pattern to take home (see page 6).

Day 3   Week 2 Philibert the First

Resources for Group Time

Vocabulary extension

Ask the children to find two words on page 10 (the first two paragraphs) that mean the same as *unhappy* (*sad, miserable*). Ask them to do the same for words that mean *happy* on page 19 (*joy, glad*).

Divide the children into two teams. One team will make a list of all the words they can find in the story that are about sadness, the other will do the same for words that are about happiness:
- *happy, glad, joy, funniest, smile, grin, chuckle, laugh*
- *sad, unhappy, miserable, gloomy, sorrowfully, unhappiness, sigh, doom, moaned, wretched, mournful.*

Encourage the children to think of other words to add to the list of *happy* words (for example *delighted, pleased, contented*). Do the same for the list of *sad* words (for example *upset, depressed, heart-broken*).

Help the children to write a sentence of their own about being happy including at least two words from the list. Repeat with a sentence about being sad.

Using a dictionary and thesaurus

Each child chooses one word from the lists they have made above and either looks up the meaning in a dictionary or finds words that mean the same in a thesaurus. Any new words that are found can be added to the lists. Children may also use a thesaurus on a word-processing program, if available.

Day 4   Week 2 Philibert the First

Resources for Group Time

Resources for Group Time
Support for Struggling Readers

Writing a setting for a story

What is the name of the place?

Describe how it looks.

What are the people (or other creatures) who live there like?

What sort of things usually happen there?

Writing composition:
Explain to the children that they are going to write a setting for a story. Encourage them to talk and plan first and to concentrate on the setting, not the action. They could either use a story of their own or a familiar one. Remind them that the readers must be able to 'make a picture' in their heads so there must be enough information and details.

Philibert the First

Word sort

These words about being happy and sad have become mixed up. Can you write them in two lists?

joy unhappiness laugh

glad miserable gloomy

smile sorrowfully delighted

unhappy chuckle overjoyed

funniest

moaned

grin

mournful

carefree

wretched

happy words	sad words

Philibert the First

Wordsearch

Find each of these words in the wordsearch square. Draw a line through each word as you find it.

miserable	grin	wretched
sad	joy	glad
smile	gloom	delighted
unhappy	overjoyed	sorrow

g	l	a	d	c	j	o	y	h
m	i	s	e	r	a	b	l	e
s	m	i	l	e	f	s	a	d
g	r	i	n	g	l	o	o	m
j	y	s	o	r	r	o	w	n
s	u	n	h	a	p	p	y	d
d	e	l	i	g	h	t	e	d
w	r	e	t	c	h	e	d	k
o	v	e	r	j	o	y	e	d

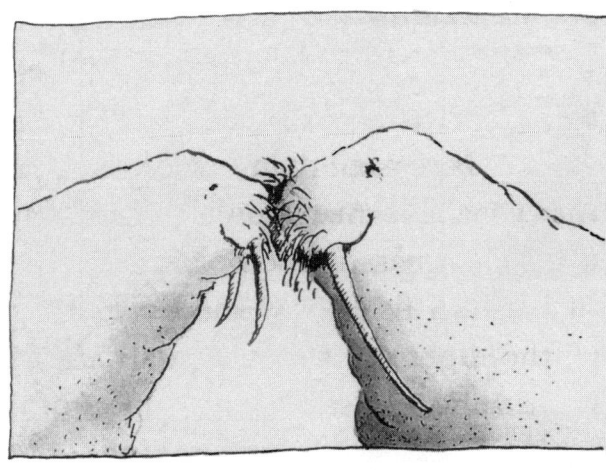

Homework

Resources for Group Time
Support for Struggling Readers

Week 3   The Hobyahs
by Val Biro

The Hobyahs are one version of the 'bogeymen' of folklore, who come secretly in the night to make off with little boys and girls, in order to eat them. As in all the best traditional tales, however, the Hobyahs never get their wicked way and all ends happily. In this account of the story, Little Girl Lucy is saved by her brave pet, Little Dog Turpie, who is more than a match for any number of Hobyahs.

The story contains many aspects of traditional stories which will be familiar to children: there is repetitive text (for example, the Hobyahs' chant) that lends itself to being read aloud, typical adult characters (the little old woman and the little old man) and the classic opening and ending for the story.

(As *The Hobyahs* does not have page numbers, you might find it helpful to use removable sticky labels to number each page. The title page would be page 1, therefore the first page of the story itself falls on page 2, and so on.)

Week 3 Objectives

	Word level	Sentence level	Text level
Day 1 Reading Traditional stories Dialogue		To use awareness of grammar, phonic and graphic knowledge, word recognition and context when reading Y3 T2 (1)	To be aware of the different voices in stories Y3 T1 (3) To investigate the style of traditional story language Y3 T2 (1)
Day 2 Comprehension Sequencing			To make sense of what they read Y2 T3 (2) To re-tell the main points of the story in sequence Y3 T3 (1)
Day 3 Sight vocabulary Spelling by analogy	Spelling by analogy with other known words Y4 T1–3 (3) To recall high frequency words Y4 T1–3 (1)		
Day 4 Contracted words Verbs – past tense	To use the apostrophe to spell shortened forms of words Y3 T2 (15)	To investigate verb tenses Y4 T1 (2)	
Day 5 Writing composition Characters			To write a character sketch Y4 T1 (11)
Homework task 1 Cloze		To predict from the text, read on, leave a gap and re-read Y2 T2 (1)	
Homework task 2 Contracted words	To use the apostrophe to spell shortened forms of words Y3 T2 (15)		

Resources for Group Time
Support for Struggling Readers

Day 1 — Week 3 The Hobyahs

Reading

The children should have already read this story with the teacher in guided reading. If they are not familiar with the book, follow the instructions for fiction books (see page 4) before beginning Day 1.

Traditional stories

Ask the children to:
- recall the opening for the story (or they can re-read it)
- repeat the above for the ending of the story
- think of other stories with similar beginnings and endings (make sure they know that these are called 'traditional' stories)
- talk, in pairs, about the characters, deciding on one word to describe each one, for example, Turpie – *brave*, Lucy – *scared*, Hobyahs – *wicked*, and so on.

Share the ideas the children have, in their pairs, and make a list together of all the words.

Reading dialogue

Encourage the children to read the first Hobyahs' chant, silently to themselves, sounding as wicked as possible.

The children should then take turns to read all the Hobyahs' chants in the text. Make sure they are reading with appropriate expression but not overdoing it! Do the same with the words of the Old Man and Old Woman, encouraging the children to express how cross they are with the barking dog.

There is no dialogue spoken by Lucy. Ask the children to imagine what she might have said as the Hobyahs put her in the sack and later when she was left hanging by the door.

Resources for Group Time

Day 2 — Week 3 The Hobyahs

Comprehension

Quiz (oral or written answers)
1. Who wanted to put the dog in the cellar?
A. The little old woman.
2. What did the Hobyahs do with their tails?
A. Swished them.
3. Where did the little old man sell Turpie?
A. The market.
4. Why did the Hobyahs stop being brave?
A. Because the dog bit off their tails.
5. What tools did the Little Old Man use to build the kennel?
A. Saw and hammer.

Quiz (written answers)
1. Who cried?
A. Lucy.
2. Where did the Hobyahs put Lucy?
A. In a sack.
3. When did the Hobyahs come to steal children?
A. In the night.
4. How did the Old Woman feel when Turpie barked?
A. Cross.
5. Who bought Turpie at the market?
A. A farmer.

Sequencing

Ask the children to retell the story, taking turns to each say a sentence and link it to the previous one (with, for example, *next night, then, later on, after that, finally*). Encourage them to be brief and to try to use their own words rather than simply reading parts of the text.

Resources for Group Time

Resources for Group Time
Support for Struggling Readers

Sight vocabulary

great, never, can't

Ask the children to find the word *great* (on page 2) and to learn to spell the word using the Look–Say–Cover–Write–Check method (see page 6 of this book) until they can write it from memory. Do the same with *never* (page 7) and *can't* (page 9). The children should write the words in their spelling books to take home for further practice.

Help the children to think of a sentence with all three words in it, and to write it down, using a coloured pencil or felt-tipped pen to highlight *great*, *never* and *can't*.

Spelling by analogy

Spelling pattern: *-le*

Ask the children to find *little* on the first few pages and look carefully at the word. They should learn to spell the word using the Look–Say–Cover–Write–Check method (see page 6) until they can write it from memory. Encourage them to think of other words that end with *-le* (for example *apple, table, muddle, kettle, wobble*). Dictate the words for the children to write in their spelling books.

Dictate the following sentences for the children to write. (Decide whether or not you want them to have the word list for reference.) Remind them about capital letters, question marks and full stops, if necessary.

*I put the **apple** on the **little** table.*
*Did the **kettle wobble**?*

The children should underline all the *-le* words in their completed sentences with a coloured pencil or felt-tipped pen. They could make word wheels or flick books with the spelling pattern to take home (see page 6).

Day 3 Week 3 The Hobyahs

Resources for Group Time

Apostrophes and contracted words

Ask the children to find *can't* (page 9). Can they think of another way to write *can't* using two words? (*Can not.*) The two words have been pushed together (or 'contracted').

Can the children say which letter has disappeared? (The *o* in *not.*) Make sure they know it has been replaced by an apostrophe.

Ask the children to find another contracted word on page 14 (*couldn't*). Do they know which two words *couldn't* is made from? (*Could not.*)

Encourage the children to tell you the contracted words for:

I am (I'm)
we are (we're)
it is (it's).

Help them to think of a few more contracted words and write them in two lists, for example: *can, can't; could, couldn't,* and so on.

Verbs

Ask the children to read the description of the Hobyahs on page 7 (*Scampering through…*)

Ask the children if they can remember what a verb is. (An 'action' word.) They should then find the verbs in the description (*scampering, swishing, shouting*). Encourage the children to notice the letters on the end of the verbs (*ing*).

Ask the children to imagine that the Hobyahs came last night. How would they have to change the verbs? (*Scampered, swished, shouted.*) Explain that these verbs are in the 'past' because they have already happened. What are the letters on the end now? (*ed*)

Help the children to find more verbs in the text. Decide if they are already in the past (for example, *barked*). If not, they should change them.

Ask the children to notice if all the verbs have the *-ed* letters on the end. Some that don't are *heard, kept, sold* and *ran*.

Day 4 Week 3 The Hobyahs

Resources for Group Time
Support for Struggling Readers

Wanted

for stealing and eating girls and boys

WARNING This creature is dangerous and should be approached with great care.

THE HOBYAH

Description: _____

_____

Where and when to find the Hobyah: _____

_____

_____

REWARD
for capture alive: _____

for information leading to arrest: _____

Please reply to: _____

_____

Day 5 — Week 3 The Hobyahs

Writing composition:
Explain to the children that they are going to make a 'wanted' poster for a Hobyah. They could draw an illustration (perhaps after they have written the poster) and should describe the Hobyah very carefully so that anyone reading it would recognize it.

The Hobyahs

Missing words

Read the story of the Hobyahs, then put the missing words (from the bottom of the page) back in the right places.

Once upon a _____, Lucy, lived with Turpie the dog, the Little _____ Woman and the Little Old Man, in a little old house in a _____ big wood. Every night the Hobyahs came _____ through the woods, shouting:

"Hobyah! Hobyah! Hobyah!
See our _____!
Let's put little Lucy in
And never _____ her back!"

But Turpie always _____ and scared them away.

The Old Woman and the Old Man were _____ with Turpie for making a noise, so they sold him to a farmer. That _____ the Hobyahs really did steal Lucy. Before they had a chance to eat her, Turpie _____ from the farmer and rescued her. He bit off all the Hobyahs' _____ and they just ran away. Lucy and Turpie ran back home and they all lived _____ ever after.

time	cross	tails	Old
sack	bring	barked	happily
scampering	great	escaped	night

The Hobyahs

Contracted words

Can you write a contracted word instead of the two words that are highlighted in each sentence? The first one has been done for you.
Don't forget the apostrophe.

1 I **can not** sleep a wink because of that barking dog.

   can't

2 We **have not** come back to pop little Lucy in our sack.

   _____

3 Turpie **could not** stay in the bedroom.

   _____

4 We **will not** let that dog get the better of us.

   _____

5 **Do not** bark so loudly, Turpie.

   _____

6 "**I am** so frightened of the Hobyahs," said Lucy.

   _____

7 **We are** going to catch the Hobyahs and put them in a sack.

   _____

8 Hobyahs **are not** very friendly.

   _____

Week 4 Instructions
Party recipes

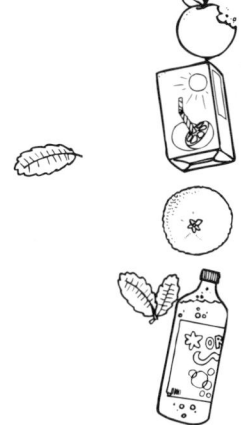

Introduction

Being able to follow instructions is an important life skill for children and the ability to give and write instructions is equally useful. Step-by-step guidelines are helpful for children who have sequencing difficulties. These two recipes (for chocolate medals and punch) provide an opportunity for children to revise the properties of instruction texts and study the particular language used (for example the imperative form of the verb).

Following the instructions in the recipes (and consuming the results) could be a reward for hard work on this week's activities! (Or the children could take the photocopied sheets home to try them out.)

Week 4 Objectives

	Word level	Sentence level	Text level
Day 1 Reading Sequencing		To use awareness of grammar, phonic and graphic knowledge, word recognition and context when reading Y3 T2 (1)	To identify features of instructional texts Y4 T1 (22)
Day 2 Comprehension Vocabulary extension	To collect new words from reading Y3 T3 (12)		To make sense of what they have read Y2 T3 (2)
Day 3 Sight vocabulary Spelling by analogy	Spelling by analogy with other known words Y4 T1–3 (3) To recall high-frequency words Y4 T1–3 (1)		
Day 4 Imperative verbs Homonyms	To explore homonyms which have the same spelling but multiple meanings Y3 T3 (14)	To understand the function of verbs in sentences Y3 T1 (3) To use the term 'verb' appropriately Y3 T1 (5)	
Day 5 Writing composition			To write clear instructions, using conventions learned from reading Y4 T1 (25)
Homework task 1 Verbs		Collect examples of verbs Y3 T1 (3)	
Homework task 2 Sentence endings		To use grammar and context when reading Y3 T2 (1)	

Reading

Before reading
Look at the layout of the text on page 43. Discuss with the children:
- why there are illustrations (to help you understand what to do)
- what else helps you to understand what to do (numbers, headings)
- why the words *very carefully* are in bold (to emphasize their importance)
- which other ways can be used to emphasize words (italic, capital letters or larger print).

Make sure the children understand the terms *recipe* and *instructions*. Read the text together. (See 'Non-fiction/information texts' on page 5.)

After reading
In pairs, the children re-read the ingredients for the fruity punch recipe.

Make a word web together showing as many ingredients as the children can remember without looking at the recipe.

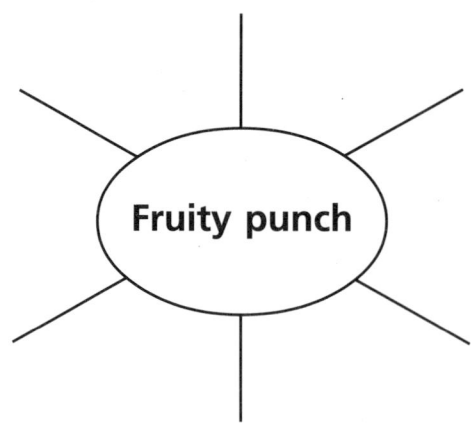

Sequencing

Let the children look at the recipe for 'Silver medals' for a couple of minutes. In turn, without looking at the text if possible, the children should repeat the instructions in their own words, trying to keep them in the correct sequence.

Encourage them to start each sentence with a verb. For example: *Pour the melted chocolate...*

Week 4 Instructions — Day 1

Resources for Group Time

Comprehension

Quiz (oral or written answers)
1. What can you use for the silver on the medals?
A. Foil.
2. How should you push the chocolate out of the cutters?
A. Very carefully.
3. Where can you melt the chocolate?
A. On the cooker or in the microwave.
4. Why does the lemonade have to go in just before you serve the fruity punch?
A. To keep its fizz.
5. What is the last thing you do to make fruity punch?
A. Stir everything together.

Quiz (written answers)
1. How many ingredients are there for the fruity punch?
A. Six.
2. Where do you put the cutters?
A. On a baking tray.
3. What is the coldest food in the recipes?
A. Ice.
4. When should you put the lemonade into the fruit punch?
A. At the end, just before serving.
5. What does *method* mean?
A. How to do it.

Vocabulary extension – word detectives

Ask the children to find and highlight (using a coloured pencil or felt-tipped pen) these words in their copy of the recipes:

segments, Ingredients, Method, substitute

Discuss with the children what they think each word means. They should write down their definitions. Ask the children to look up one or two words each in a dictionary and compare the definitions with their own.

Week 4 Instructions — Day 2

Resources for Group Time

Sight vocabulary

until, leave, together

Ask the children to find the word *until* (in the recipe for 'Silver medals') and to learn to spell the word using the Look–Say–Cover–Write–Check method (see page 6) until they can write it from memory. Do the same with *Leave* (in 'Silver medals') and *together* (in 'Fruity punch'). The children should write the words in their spelling books to take home for further practice.

Help the children to think of a sentence with all three words in it and to write it down, using a coloured pencil or felt-tipped pen to highlight *until, leave* and *together*.

Spelling by analogy

Spelling pattern: *ge-*

Ask the children to find *gently* (in 'Silver medals') and to look carefully at the word. They should learn to spell the word using the Look–Say–Cover–Write–Check method (see page 6) until they can write it from memory.

Ask them what the letter *g* at the beginning of *gentle* sounds like (*j*). Encourage them to think of other words that sound like *j* but begin with *ge* (for example, *gents, Germany, gel, gem, general, genie, George, germ*). Dictate the words for the children to write in their spelling books.

Dictate the following sentences for the children to write. (Decide whether or not you want them to have the word list for reference.) Remind them about capital letters, question marks and full stops, if necessary.

*The **German general** went into the **gents**.*
***George** liked to put **gel** on his hair.*

The children should underline all the *ge-* words in their completed sentences with a coloured pencil or felt-tipped pen. They could make word wheels or flick books with the spelling pattern to take home (see page 6).

Day 3 — Week 4 Instructions

Verbs – commands

Ask the children if they can remember what a verb is (an 'action' word). Help them to underline all the verbs in the recipe for 'Silver medals' (*Break, Put, stand, heat, Stir, melted, Pour, Leave, Push, Wrap, Cut, go, Stick*).

Encourage the children to notice where the verbs occur (mostly at the beginning of each instruction).

Each of those verbs is telling the reader to do something. These verbs are commands (the correct term is *imperative*). Tell the children they are 'bossy' verbs. Ask the children to think of some more 'bossy' verbs. What do their parents tell them to do? (*Brush* your teeth. *Say* hello to Grandma. *Turn* the TV off and so on.)

Help the children to write three sentences, each of which begins with a bossy *verb*.

Words with different meanings

Ask the children to find the word *punch* in the recipe. Can they think of another meaning for *punch*?

Look at the following words in the recipes and help the children to think of another meaning for each word:

bowl – as in cricket
cool – fashionable
set – a collection
stand – in a sports stadium, a hat-stand, 'I can't *stand* this'
stick – a piece of wood
orange – the colour
chop – meat
leaves – goes away

Day 4 — Week 4 Instructions

Game instructions

How to play _____

You will need: _____

_____

How to play: _____

_____
_____
_____
_____
_____
_____
_____
_____
_____
_____
_____

Writing composition:
Explain to the children that they are going to write the instructions for a game they know well. They need to write very clearly, as if they are explaining it to a child who does not know anything about the game. Encourage them to start each instruction with a verb.

Instructions

Find the verbs

Find the verbs in this recipe and colour them. (Remember: a verb is an action word.)

1   Pour the flour into a bowl.

2   Crack the eggs and beat them with a whisk.

3   Add the egg mixture to the flour.

4   Put in a pinch of salt.

5   Measure two tablespoons of sugar.

6   Add the sugar to the mixture in the bowl.

7   Mix everything together until it is smooth.

8   Heat a little butter in a frying pan.

9   Pour a half-cup of the mixture into the pan and turn the pan until it covers the bottom.

10 Lift the edge to see if it is a golden colour underneath.

11 Toss the _____ to turn it over.

12 Heat the other side until it is cooked.

What is the missing word? _____

Resources for Group Time
Support for Struggling Readers

Sort the sentence endings

The sentences in this recipe have the wrong endings.
Can you sort them out? Write the correct endings below.

1. Wash the mint | (except for the core).
2. Peel the apple | before adding the lemonade and ice.
3. Chop the apple into small chunks | and pull the leaves away from the stalks.
4. Divide the orange into segments | into a large glass bowl or jug.
5. Put the pieces of fruit | to mix everything together.
6. Stir the punch gently | and cut the segments up.
7. Wait until you are ready to serve the punch | and orange.

1. Wash the mint _____

2. Peel the apple _____

3. Chop the apple into small chunks _____

4. Divide the orange into segments _____

5. Put the pieces of fruit _____

6. Stir the punch gently _____

7. Wait until you are ready to serve the punch _____

Week 5 Concrete poetry

'Orange' and 'Pineapple' by John Cotton, 'Earth-worm' by Leonard Clark, 'Inside the egg' by Noel Petty

Concrete poetry helps children see and hear how words can be 'shaped', literally, to create particular effects. The wriggling shape of the 'Earth-worm' poem forms an obvious contrast with the smooth sphere of 'Inside the egg'. Three of the poems ('Orange', 'Pineapple' and 'Inside the egg') are written in the first person, and the fourth, 'Earth-worm', expresses the poet's friendly opinion of worms.

Writing their own shape poems gives children an opportunity to express a personal viewpoint and can encourage a more informal and imaginative response to the subject.

Week 5 Objectives

	Word level		
Day 1 Reading	To use phonic/spelling, graphic, grammatical and contextual knowledge as a cue when reading Y4 T2 (1)		To compare and contrast poems on similar themes Y4 T1 (7) To express views about a poem Y3 T1 (8)
Day 2 Comprehension Rhyme			To make sense of what they read Y2 T3 (2) To identify patterns of rhyme Y4 T2 (7)
Day 3 Sight vocabulary Spelling by analogy	Spelling by analogy with other known words Y4 T1–3 (3) To recall high-frequency words Y4 T1–3 (1)		
Day 4 Syllables Vocabulary	To collect new words, infer the meaning and use dictionaries to check Y3 T2 (17–19)		To count the syllables in lines of poetry Y4 T3 (5)
Day 5 Writing composition			To write poems, experimenting with different forms Y4 T3 (14)
Homework task 1 Cloze		To use context and predict from the text when reading Y3 T3 (1)	
Homework task 2 Comprehension		To use awareness of grammar and context when reading Y3 T2 (1)	

Day 1 — Week 5 Concrete poetry

Reading

Each child will need a copy of the four poems (see pages 44–46).

Ask the children which of the four poems they think could be grouped together ('Orange' and 'Pineapple').

'Orange' and 'Pineapple'

Ask the children to read 'Orange' silently, then together as a group. Discuss what they think *succulent* means? (Juicy.) They should use a dictionary to check.

Now read 'Pineapple' together. Discuss with the children whose voice is speaking in each poem. Encourage the children to find words to show this (*I, me my*).

In pairs, ask the children:
- to talk about the ways in which the two poems are the same (They are both about fruit, written in the first person, have four lines and rhyme.)
- what part of the fruit is described first, in each poem (the outside; what it looks like)
- to decide if the poet likes oranges and pineapples and highlight the words in the poems that tell you he does (for example *beauty, sweet, treat* and so on).

'Earth-worm' and 'Inside the egg'

Ask the children:
- to describe the shapes of these two poems before they read them
- to suggest why the lines are of different lengths in 'Earth-worm' (to make the poem 'wriggle' like a worm.)
- why 'Inside the egg' does not have separate verses with space in between.

Read 'Earth-worm' aloud, together. Ask the children which word means 'wriggle'. (*Squirm.*) Why did the poem use the word *squirm*? (It rhymes with *worm*.)

Read 'Inside the egg' aloud, together. Ask the children who is speaking in 'Inside the egg'. (The chick.)

The children should choose their two favourite poems (one 'fruit' poem and either 'Inside the egg' or 'Earth-worm') and practise reading them aloud to each other.

Resources for Group Time

Day 2 — Week 5 Concrete poetry

Comprehension

Quiz (oral or written answers)
1. Whose face is rough and scaly?
A. Pineapple.
2. Who is surprised to be alone?
A. The chick inside the egg.
3. Why does the poet not squirm when he sees a worm?
A. He likes worms.
4. What does the poet think you should eat with pineapple?
A. Ice cream.
5. What rhymes with *squirm* in the poem?
A. Worm.

Quiz (written answers)
1. What is the pineapple's hair like?
A. A punk's.
2. Which fruit is like the sun?
A. Orange.
3. What was the chick's good idea?
A. To peck.
4. Who has no eyes in its face?
A. A worm.
5. Can an earth-worm hear?
A. No.

Rhymes and spelling

Ask the children to find the rhyming words in 'Earth-worm' and colour them. Make sure they include the lines with single words.

The children should write the rhyming words in two lists, one for rhymes with the same spelling pattern (for example *hat, fat, that*) and a second list of words that rhyme but are spelled differently (for example *worm, squirm* and *half, laugh*).

Resources for Group Time

Resources for Group Time
Support for Struggling Readers

Sight vocabulary

half, suddenly, eyes

Ask the children to find the word *half* (in 'Earth-worm') and to learn to spell the word using the Look–Say–Cover–Write–Check method (see page 6) until they can write it from memory. Do the same with *suddenly* and *eyes* (both in 'Earth-worm'). The children should write the words in their spelling books to take home for further practice.

Help the children to think of a sentence with all three words in it, and to write it down, using a coloured pencil or felt-tipped pen to highlight *half*, *suddenly* and *eyes*.

Spelling by analogy

Spelling pattern: *wor-*

Ask the children to find *worm* in 'Earth-worm' and look carefully at the word. They should learn to spell *worm* using the Look–Say–Cover–Write–Check method (see page 6) until they can write it from memory. Make sure they notice that the *-or-* in *worm* sounds like *-er-*. Encourage them to think of more words that start with *wor-* (for example *word, worse, world, work, worth*). Dictate the words for the children to write in their spelling books.

Dictate the following sentences for the children to write. (Decide whether or not you want them to have the word list for reference.) Remind them about capital letters, question marks and full stops, if necessary.

*That is the **worst** joke in the **world**. Can you **work** hard and spell **words** like **worm**?*

The children should underline all the *wor-* words in their completed sentences with a coloured pencil or felt-tipped pen. They could make word wheels or flick books with the spelling pattern to take home (see page 6).

Resources for Group Time

Day 3 — Week 5 Concrete poetry

Syllables

Ask the children to find the shortest and longest lines in 'Inside the egg' and count the syllables in each one. (Remind them that a syllable is one 'beat', not necessarily one word.)

Shortest line: *Hello*, or *Peck! Peck!* (two syllables).
Longest line: *I thought I wouldn't live quite alone* or *I've not lost heart, I'm not dejected* (nine syllables).

Do the same with 'Earth-worm'.

Shortest line: There are many one-word lines in this poem.
Longest line: *is really rather clever* or *you wouldn't like to come out* (seven syllables).

Each child, in turn, secretly chooses a line in 'Pineapple' and claps the syllables. The others guess which line it was.

Vocabulary extension

You will need dictionaries for this activity.

Divide the children into two teams (the 'Inside the egg' team and the 'Earth-worm' team) to play 'word detectives'. Give each team three words from their poem:
- 'Earth-worm' team – *squirm, shrink, toil*.
- 'Inside the egg' team – *dejected, universe, extend*.

The children find and highlight each word in their copies of the poems and discuss what they think they mean, then write down their definitions. Using a dictionary, the children look up the words and compare the definitions with their own.

Resources for Group Time

Day 4 — Week 5 Concrete poetry

Support for Struggling Readers

No longer a caterpillar

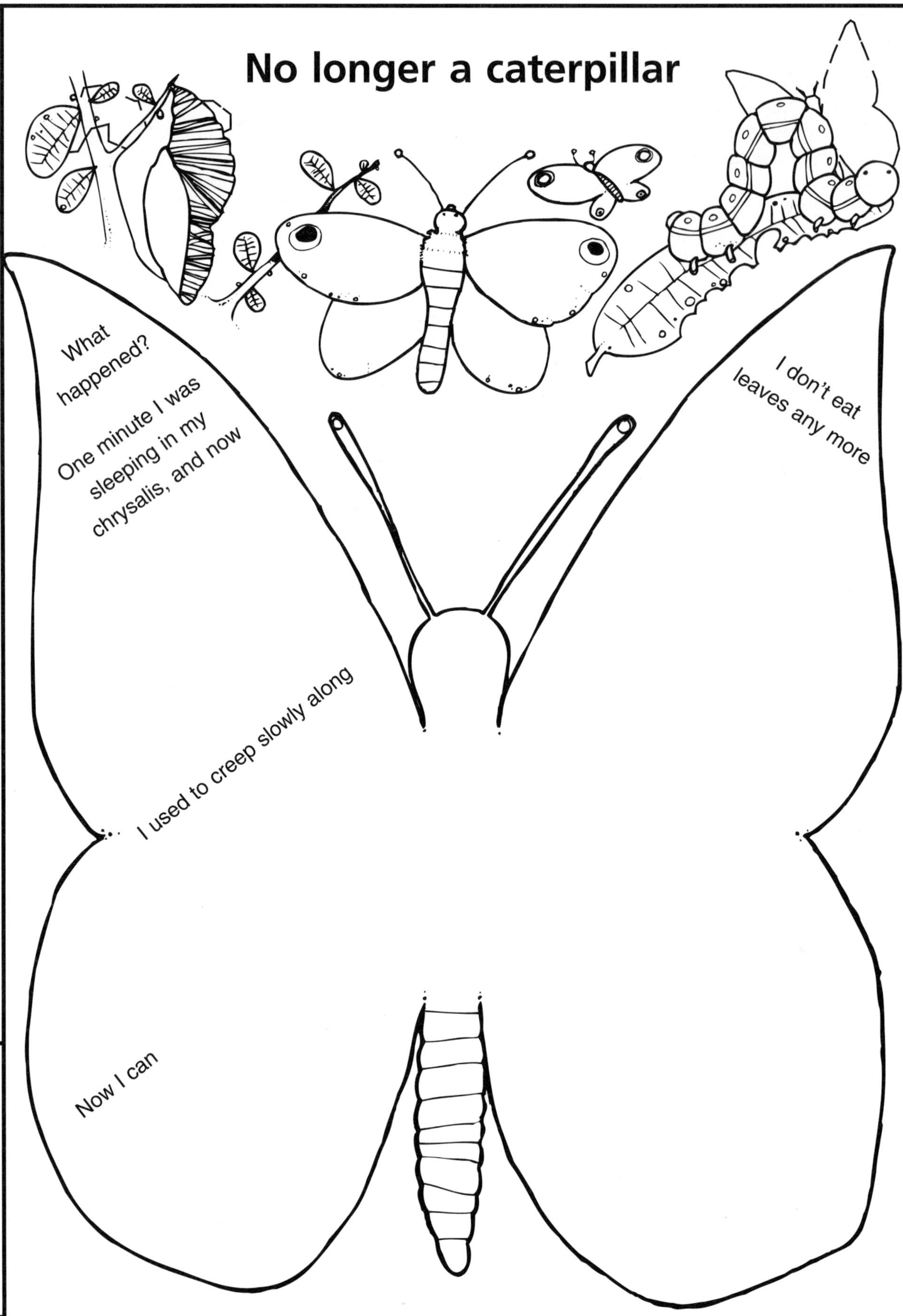

What happened? One minute I was sleeping in my chrysalis, and now

I don't eat leaves any more

I used to creep slowly along

Now I can

Week 5 Concrete poetry

Day 5

Writing composition:
Encourage the children to write their own shape poem in the style of 'Inside the egg'. They should write in the first person (as if they are the butterfly). They can choose whether or not to use rhyme.

Concrete poetry

Fruit poems

Read the poems, then put the missing words back in the right places.

Orange

I am a bright _____ orange

Quite _____-like in my beauty,

Peel off my _____ and then you'll find

Me succulent _____ fruity.

Pineapple

My face may be _____ and quite scaly,

And my _____'s a bit like a punk's

But _____ I'm sweet and a bit of a treat,

With ice _____ and cut up in chunks.

rough   sun   inside   and
cream   round   skin   hair

Concrete poetry

Poem jumble

The lines from these poems have become jumbled up. Can you write them in the correct order?

Orange
I am a bright round orange
And my hair's a bit like a punk's
Peel off my skin and then you'll find
But inside I'm sweet and a bit of a treat,

Pineapple
My face may be rough and quite scaly,
Me succulent and fruity.
With ice cream and cut up in chunks.
Quite sun-like in my beauty,

Orange

_____
_____
_____
_____

Pineapple

_____
_____
_____
_____

Week 6 Explanation text

Air pressure and windy weather
(from *Weather and Climate* by Barbara Taylor)

Reading non-fiction texts is an important strand throughout the Literacy Hour work in Key Stage 2. Boys, who statistically are more likely to be struggling readers, often respond more enthusiastically to the reading task when the text is non-fiction.

This information text explains in straightforward and understandable language what air pressure means and what happens when the wind blows. The layout of the text is typical of non-fiction and uses illustrations and captions to explain the processes. The examples relate to the everyday experience of children and will help them to grasp the information in the text more easily.

Week 6 Objectives

	Word level	Sentence level	Text level
Day 1 Reading		To use awareness of grammar, phonic and graphic knowledge, word recognition and context when reading Y3 T2 (1)	To prepare for factual research Y4 T2 (16)
Day 2 Comprehension Key words			To make sense of what they read Y2 T3 (2) To locate key words and mark extracts Y4 T2 (17 & 18)
Day 3 Sight vocabulary Spelling by analogy	Spelling by analogy with other known words Y4 T1–3 (3) To recall high-frequency words Y4 T1–3 (1)		
Day 4 Singular and plural	To investigate and identify basic rules for changing the spelling of nouns when *s* is added Y3 T2 (9)	To use the terms singular and plural appropriately Y3 T2 (5)	
Day 5 Writing composition			To make a simple record of information from text read Y3 T1 (22)
Homework task 1 Alphabetical order	To organise words alphabetically, using the first two letters Y3 T2 (23)		
Homework task 2 Singular and plural		Recognise the use of singular and plural forms Y3 T2 (4)	

Resources for Group Time
Support for Struggling Readers

Reading

Before reading

Before looking at the extract on photocopiable pages 47–8, tell the children they are going to be reading a text that *explains* how something happens or works. Begin the KWL grid (see below). The children will need an A4-size version of the grid.

What do I already know?	What do I want to find out?	What have I learned?

K = What do I already **k**now?
W = What do I **w**ant to find out?
L = What have I **l**earned?

To help the children to complete the first two columns of the KWL grid:
- Ask, 'What do you already know about the wind?' Encourage them to write two pieces of information in the first column.
- Help them to think of two questions about the wind. They should then write their questions in the second column.
- Give the children a few minutes to look through the extract and enjoy the illustrations, before reading it. Now read the text together (see 'Non-fiction/information texts' on page 5).

After reading

The children can complete the third column of the KWL grid by writing two facts they have learned from the text.

Day 1 — Week 6 Explanation text

Comprehension

Quiz (oral or written answers)

1. What is air pressure?
A. The weight of the air pressing down on the Earth.
2. What does a weather vane tell you?
A. Where the wind is blowing from.
3. Is air pressure high or low at the top of a mountain?
A. Low.
4. What always blows from high to low pressure?
A. Wind.
5. At what number on the Beaufort Scale do flags flap?
A. 3.

Quiz (written answers)

1. What did the people of China use to measure wind, long ago?
A. Kites.
2. What is the highest number for the strongest wind on the Beaufort Scale?
A. 12.
3. The wind blowing is like letting the air out of a _____.
A. Balloon.
4. Where might the air pressure make your ears hurt?
A. In a plane.
5. How can the wind make electricity?
A. Windmills.

Finding key words

Look again at the first part of the extract: 'Air pressure'.

Tell the children they are gong to decide which are the most important words in the extract. Help them to highlight or underline (using the same colour) no more than about six key words which tell the reader about air pressure.

Encourage the children to share their results to see if they agree about which are the key words.

Day 2 — Week 6 Explanation text

Sight vocabulary

earth, across, balloon

Ask the children to find the word *Earth* (in 'Air pressure') and to learn to spell the word using the Look–Say–Cover–Write–Check method (see page 6) until they can write it from memory. Do the same with *across* and *balloon* (in 'Windy weather'). The children should write the words in their spelling books to take home for further practice.

Help the children to think of a sentence with all three words in it, and to write it down, using a coloured pencil or felt-tipped pen to highlight *Earth, across* and *balloon*.

Spelling by analogy

Spelling pattern: -eep

Ask the children to find *sweep* in 'Windy weather' and to look carefully at the word. They should learn to spell the word using the Look–Say–Cover–Write–Check method (see page 6) until they can write it from memory. Encourage them to think of other words that rhyme with *sweep* but only write down those words that have the same spelling pattern (in other words, not *heap* or *cheap* and so on). Suitable words are *creep, deep, keep, peep, sleep, sheep* and *weep*. Dictate the words for the children to write in their spelling books.

Dictate the following sentences for the children to write. (Decide whether or not you want them to have the word list for reference.) Remind them about capital letters, question marks and full stops, if necessary.

*Do **sheep weep** if they cannot **sleep**?*
*I **keep** trying to **sweep** up the **deep** snow.*

The children should underline all the *-eep* words in their completed sentences with a coloured pencil or felt-tipped pen. They could make word wheels or flick books with the spelling pattern to take home (see page 6).

Week 6 Explanation text — Day 3

Singular and plural

Ask the children if they know what *singular* means. (Tell them it is like *single* if they cannot remember.)

When they know that *singular* means 'one of something', ask them if they know what *plural* means. (More than one, whether it refers to two or to millions.)

Ask the children if they can find a plural word in the first sentence in the 'Air pressure' extract (*ears*). Help them to find more examples of words in the plural in the extract (for example, *eardrums, changes, mountains*) and to notice how each plural word ends (letter *s*).

Plural words that change their spelling (*y* and *ies*)

Ask the children to read the 'Eye spy' section of 'Air pressure' and find the word *body*. Find the plural of *baby* in the extract (*bodies*). Make sure they notice what has happened to the spelling. (The *y* disappears and is replaced by *ies*.)

Now ask the children to look for the word *enemies* in the caption to the kites illustration in 'Windy weather'. Ask them to spell *enemy*. Dictate other words that end with *-y* for the children to write in a list: *lady, fairy, study, copy, reply, fly, spy*. They should write the plural word next to each singular word, for example:

lady   ladies

Encourage the children to write sentences using some of the plural words.

Week 6 Explanation text — Day 4

Resources for Group Time
Support for Struggling Readers

Air pressure and the wind

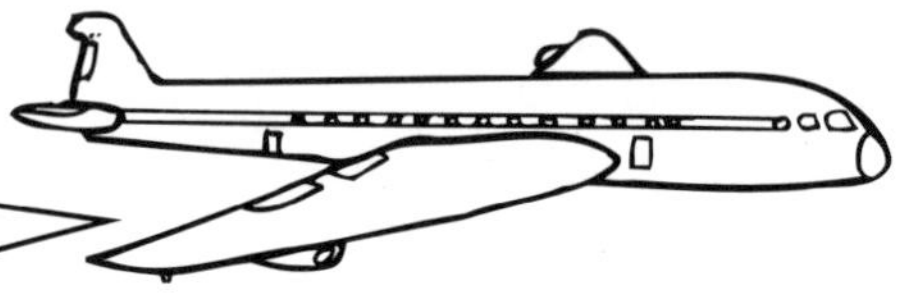

Writing composition:
Explain to the children that they are going to write titles and captions for the illustrations so that other children will understand about air pressure and the wind. They should try to write two sentences of explanation for each picture. They may want to re-read some of the text first but make sure they do not copy from the text. They should write the information in their own words.

Explanation text

Alphabetical order

Can you write these words about air pressure and wind in alphabetical order? Be careful, some of them start with the same letter. Remember to look at the second letter to put them in order.

	Alphabetical order
plane	*air*
changes	
kite	
pressure	
air	
weather	
strength	
machines	
flag	
two	
important	
high	
windy	
day	
balloon	

Homework

Resources for Group Time
Support for Struggling Readers

Explanation text

Singular and plural

Some of these words are singular (meaning just one) and some are plural (more than one) but they have become mixed up. Write them in two lists. Be careful! Some plural words do not end with the letter **s**.

mountain   levels   feet   children   babies

enemy   differences   change   balloons   winds   bus

mice   machines   class   planes   Singular

Plural	

Instructions for party recipes

You will need:
- a bar of plain chocolate
- round cutters (for cutting pastry)
- a baking tray
- silver foil
- ribbon (or coloured string)
- sticky tape

How to make the medals
1. Break the chocolate into pieces.
2. Put the pieces of chocolate into a bowl.
3. Either: stand the bowl in a saucepan of hot water and heat gently on the cooker
   or: put the bowl into the microwave.
4. Stir the chocolate until it has melted.
5. Put the round cutters on the baking tray.
6. Pour the melted chocolate into each cutter until it is about ½cm thick.
7. Leave the tray in a cool place until it has set hard.
8. Push the chocolate circles **very carefully** out of the cutters.
9. Wrap each chocolate medal in silver foil.
10. Cut a length of ribbon or string for each medal (long enough to go over your head easily).
11. Stick the ends of the ribbon or string onto the back of each medal with sticky tape.

Fruity punch

Serves 8

Ingredients
- lemonade (1 litre)
- pure fruit juice (1 litre)
- ice
- mint
- 1 apple
- 1 orange (or 2 clementines)

Method
1. Wash the mint and pull the leaves away from the stalks.
2. Peel the apple and orange (or clementines).
3. Chop the apple into small chunks (except for the core).
4. Divide the orange into segments and cut the segments up.
5. Put the pieces of fruit into a large glass bowl or jug.
6. Add the mint leaves.
7. Wait until you are ready to serve the punch before adding the lemonade and ice.
8. Stir the punch gently to mix everything together.

If you don't like fizzy drinks, you could substitute more fruit juice for the lemonade.

Orange

I am a bright round orange
Quite sun-like in my beauty,
Peel off my skin
 and then you'll find
Me succulent and fruity.

John Cotton

Pineapple

My face may be rough
 and quite scaly,
And my hair's a bit like
 a punk's,
But inside I'm sweet
 and a bit of a treat,
With ice cream
 and cut up in chunks.

John Cotton

Earth-worm

Leonard Clark

Do you squirm when you see
an earth-worm?
I never do squirm I think
because I think
a big fat worm clever
is really it can shrink
the way and go
so small
without
a sound
into the ground.
And then
what about
all
that work it does
and no oxygen
or miner's hat?
Marvellous to admit,
you have don't like fat
even if worms a bit,
pink with that
how it thin

slippery skin
it makes its way
day after day
through the soil,
such honest toil.
And don't forget
the dirt, I bet
it eats, I bet
it wouldn't like to come out
you ought to squirt
at night to squirm
it all over the place
with no eyes in your face.
I doubt if you know
too if you know is deaf, but
an earth-worm YOU go
it can hear
to and fro
even if you cut
it in half.
So not laugh
do squirm
or squirm
again
when
you
suddenly
see
a worm.

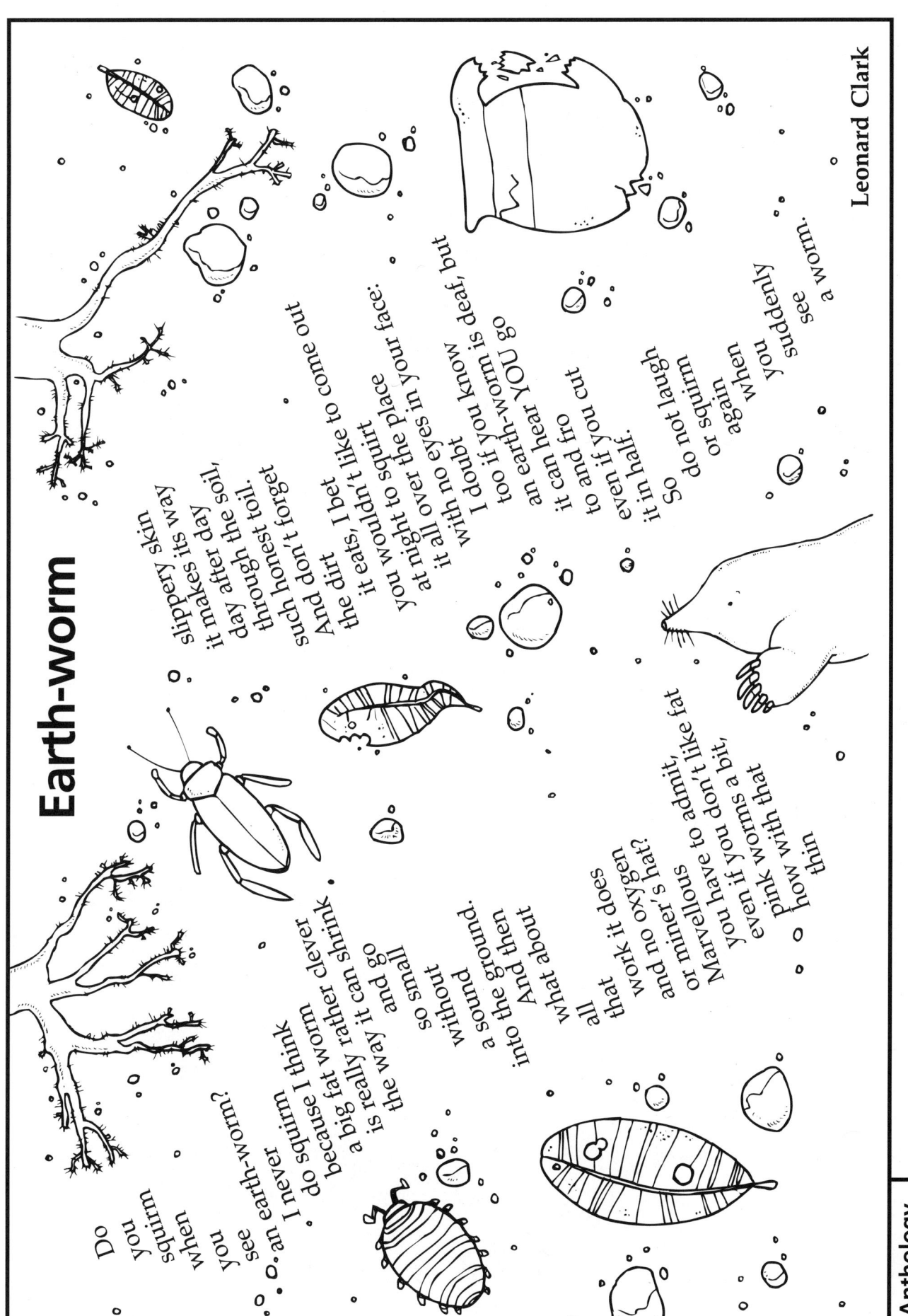

Inside the egg

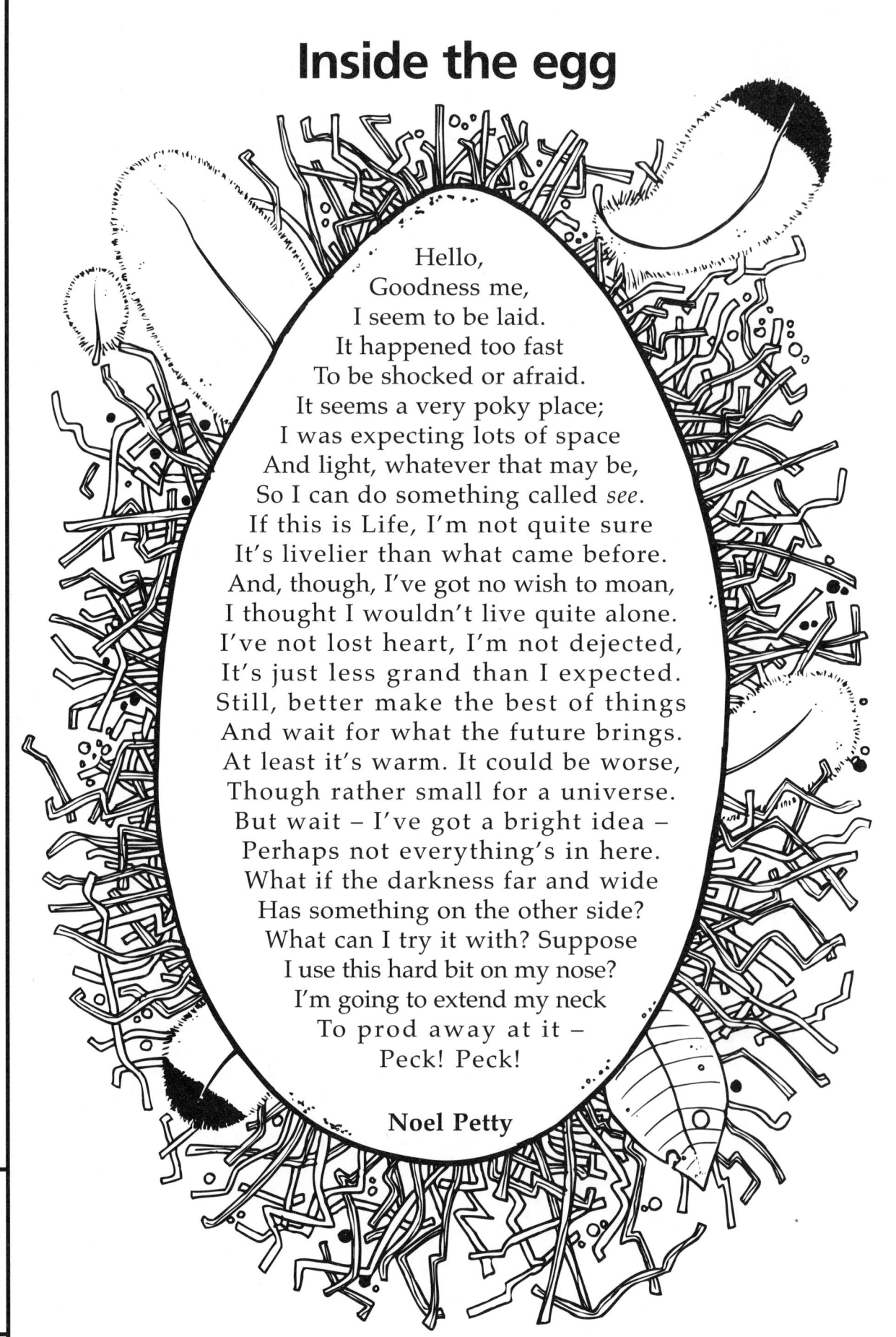

Hello,
Goodness me,
I seem to be laid.
It happened too fast
To be shocked or afraid.
It seems a very poky place;
I was expecting lots of space
And light, whatever that may be,
So I can do something called *see*.
If this is Life, I'm not quite sure
It's livelier than what came before.
And, though, I've got no wish to moan,
I thought I wouldn't live quite alone.
I've not lost heart, I'm not dejected,
It's just less grand than I expected.
Still, better make the best of things
And wait for what the future brings.
At least it's warm. It could be worse,
Though rather small for a universe.
But wait – I've got a bright idea –
Perhaps not everything's in here.
What if the darkness far and wide
Has something on the other side?
What can I try it with? Suppose
I use this hard bit on my nose?
I'm going to extend my neck
To prod away at it –
    Peck! Peck!

Noel Petty

Air pressure

When you take off or land in an aircraft, your ears may hurt or feel uncomfortable. This is because your eardrums can feel changes in air pressure as the aircraft moves quickly up and down. But what is air pressure? It is caused by the weight of all the air in the atmosphere pressing down on Earth. Air pressure changes with height and also when air warms up or cools down. Changes in air pressure cause changes in the weather.

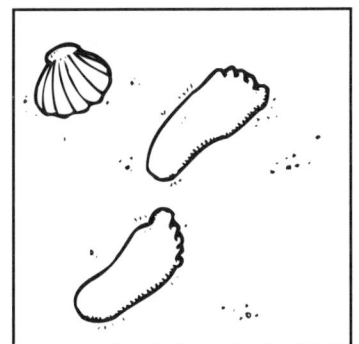

Eye spy

Have you ever noticed how your feet sink into wet sand because of the pressure caused by the weight of your body? We do not usually notice air pressure, though, because the air inside our bodies presses outwards and this cancels the effect of the air pressing against the outside of our bodies.

Windy weather

When the wind blows, it is rather like letting air out of a balloon. The air inside the balloon is at high pressure and it rushes out to where the pressure is lower. Winds all over the world are caused by differences in temperature and pressure, and they always blow from high to low pressure areas. Some winds that blow regularly in just one area have a special name, like the cold Mistral wind in southern France. Other winds sweep across the whole Earth.

Thousands of years ago, the Chinese flew kites to frighten their enemies or to measure the power of the wind. Today, we fly kites mainly as toys.

Windmills at work

As the wind pushes the sails of these windmills round, they make electricity. This way of making energy does not pollute, or dirty, the environment.

The two most important things about the wind are its strength or speed and the direction in which it is blowing. We use a weather vane or a windsock (a kind of long cloth tube through which the wind is funnelled) to see wind direction. Wind strength is measured by the Beaufort Scale, windsocks or by special scientific instruments called anemometers. These machines have several small cups that spin when caught in the wind. The speed of the spin is then measured against a scale.

The Beaufort Scale is used to describe wind strength. It has 12 numbers, ranging from calm to a violent storm or hurricane.

| 1 smoke drifts | 3 flags flap | 5 small waves on water | 7 hard to walk | 10/11 trees uprooted |
| 2 leaves rustle | 4 paper blows | 6 umbrellas blow inside out | 8/9 tiles blown off roofs | 12 buildings destroyed |